# Windthrow & Salvage

# Windthrow & Salvage

Poems by

Randall R. Freisinger

Cover design by Shay Culligan

Cover art: William Blake (1757-1827), "The Lord Answering Job from the Whirlwind" (date unknown). Permission granted by the National Galleries of Scotland and the trustees of Mr. Graham Robertson in 1949 through the Art Fund.

ISBN: 978-1-949229-69-1

Kelsay Books Inc.

kelsaybooks.com

502 S 1040 E. A119
American Fork, Utah 84003

Windthrow *refers to a powerful downburst of high wind during a strong thunderstorm that causes severe damage to a forest.*

*****

*Salvage operations reclaim whatever value remains in such storm-damaged timber.*

*for Jill*

*And in memory of Bill Kloefkorn*
*1932-2011*
*State Poet of Nebraska*
*The Better Maker and Muse*

# Acknowledgments

Thanks to the following periodicals in whose pages these poems, sometimes in slightly different versions, first were published:

Ambassador Poetry Project: “Those Who Can, Do”; *Atlanta Review:* “Taking No Prisoners”; *Black Warrior Review:* “Word Games”; *Bridge Eight:* “The Telemachus Gene,” “The Fisher King At The Mayo Clinic,” “Hamlet: A Revision,” “Dream Girl,” “Roland Redux”; *Calliope:* “The Drinker,” “Dancing School”; *The Chariton Review:* “First Dibs,” “Daisy”; *Green Mountain Review:* “Red Light, Green Light”; *Laurel Review:* “Slow-Pitch Tournament, Alston, Michigan”; *The Michigan Poet:* “Wait For Me”; *Nebraska Review:* “Hurricane Season”; *New Collage:* “Radical Mastectomy”; *New Letters:* “Cursing The Deaf,” “My Father’s Hands,” “So This Is Sex”; *ONE: An Online Magazine (Jacar Press):* “Our World”; *Pank*: “Grass,” “Retired From Television, The Sex Therapist Explains”; *Pike Creek Review:* “Graffiti”; *Relief: A Journal Of Art And Faith:* “Dickering With God”; *South Carolina Review:* “Another Day,” “Home Movies,” “Waterfront Concert,” “The Rehearsal”; *Sugar House Review:* “Alien Sex,” “I Hear Voices In A Book Shop In Duluth, Minnesota,” “The Recovery Room,” “Cherry Thieves,” “Seizing The Day,” “Revenge”; *Third Wednesday:* “Audition”; *Xavier Review:* “*Ex Post Facto:* Rhetoric 101.”

Thanks also to Wayne State University Press, where "At The Bishop Baraga Shrine" and "Boating To The Dreamland Bar And Grill" initially appeared in *The Way North: Collected Upper Peninsula New Works,* edited by Ron Riekki (2013).

"The Runaway" and "Girl At Mirror" first appeared in the chapbook *Nostalgia's Thread: Ten Poems on Norman Rockwell Painting*s (Hol Art Books, 2009).

"Slow-Pitch Softball Tournament, Alston, Michigan" was also included in a chapbook entitled *Hand Shadows* (Green Tower Press, 1998).

"Red Light, Green Light" has been reprinted in the *1997 Anthology of Magazine Verse & Yearbook of American Poetry* (Monitor Books) and in *Comedy in Contemporary American Poetry* (Green Mountain Review, Anniversary Issue, 2002).

# Contents

II Salvage

# Gale Warning

*And here I am my own extinction in sight and*
*Everything still such a screwup.*
—C.K. Williams, "Timeline," in *Writers Writing Dying: Poems*

November: gale season here, up north,
by the whip-lashed shores of Lake Superior.
Edmund Fitzgerald weather, thirty-foot waves,
water so deep and cold dead sailors' bodies
bob amidst the wreckage, so well preserved
they might begin to chant a sea shanty, or so lake
lore has it. November: stormy times, too,
in the body politic. Unexpected headwinds,
we say. Mistakes in navigation, we admit.
No rescue can come of this, we agree.
Only debris. Then, with luck, recovery.
We say such things to prop up truths
refusing to fit in the beveled box of Reason.

A guy I know at the gym died last week.
Fitness freak. Years younger. In his locker
workout clothes hang limp where he left them
after his last hour on the stationary bike.
Shoes. Soap. Shampoo. Razor. A large jar
of protein powder for lean muscles
he won't anymore flex. Hung from a vent hole
in his locker door, a pair of cheap reading
glasses needed for seeing his combination.
I tell my wife his locker was next to mine.
*I hope it isn't contagious,* she says, a joke,
which death mostly is with its poor timing,
a punch line that often leaves us groaning.

Science says we're in the midst of a sixth
great extinction. Ripley says, *Believe it or not.*
Simon says, *Tally them.* Giraffes, elephants,
black rhinos, sea turtles, lowland gorillas,
Siberian cranes, bumble bees, to name
just a few. Ice melt. Sea rise. Bleached coral
reefs. The Dead Sea now really dying, drying up,
and the Sea of Galilee, storied stomping ground
of Jesus: shrinking, it too about to vanish.
An omen, some assure us, of Christ's return.
A sign, claim others, of the Antichrist, hero
of *Midnight,* sequel to *High Noon,* arriving
soon at theaters everywhere. No plaintive tune
this time by Frankie Lane to grace the credits.
Just a laugh track and cameras panning back
and forth between the Clock and us, a clueless,
bootless mob of extras milling about in the dust,
waiting for someone, anyone to cry *Cut!*

# I

# Windthrow

*But ah, but O thou terrible, why wouldst thou rude on me*
*Thy wring-world right foot rock? Lay a lionlimb against me? scan*
*With darksome devouring eyes my bruisèd bones? and fan,*
*O in turns of tempest, me heaped there; me frantic to avoid thee and flee?*

—Gerard Manley Hopkins, "Carrion Comfort"

# Cursing The Deaf

*Thou shall not curse the deaf, nor put a stumbling block*
*before the blind, but shall fear thy God.*
—Leviticus 19

When they shipped them to our school,
at first it was good for the class
cut-ups, who could mimic the shrill,
almost hysterical pitch of their voices
when, excited, they forsook the language
of hands for the fuller register of the human
tongue. We would stagger with laughter
at recess, our mock castrato improvisations
leaving our friends doubled over, shrieking
with delight. It was midway through
the 1950s, and we were pure, flawless
products of the American century.
These sudden intruders seemed normal
enough until their talking hands betrayed
them or a skein of inarticulate sounds
escaped their mouths and marked them
as clearly as the Negro cleaning women
blue-black as used oil who shuffled tiredly
up and down the sidewalks of our segregated
neighborhood. When the deaf boys began
to move in on our girlfriends, we fought
them after school, their fists to our surprise
articulate, their hatred eloquent.
Our teachers tried to help us torture
our fingers into meaningful figures
of truce, but in our lexicon it was treason
to speak to the enemy so we pressed on
and finally succeeded in driving them back
to wherever the deaf belonged.

At home, on another front, war lingered.
Some nights that year I'd stuff wads of cotton
deep into my ears to keep from hearing
the ack-ack of bitter words below,
or I'd muffle the sounds of ambush, hiding
beneath the headset of my crystal radio
and listening to rock n' roll on a station
in distant Del Rio, Texas, which advertised
autographed pictures of Jesus Christ.
On such nights I sometimes wished
I could be like one of those kids
we had vanquished, adrift on a stream of
silence, free of the collateral damage
of words. Before sleep, when I prayed
my rote mechanical Now I Lay Me, part
of my heart already believed in a God
who must be deaf, or too far removed
to read the world's lips, or just
too stubborn to give us a sign.

# Red Light, Green Light

It was a game, a reprise
of the one with Mother, the way
you would edge each day farther
up or down your street, increasing
the distance, testing limits, waiting for her
to say *Enough!* Because you played
by the rules, when you found yourself
in the dark with a girl, you waited for her
to whisper *green.* Then and only

then could your tongue, authorized, try
for something vaguely known as *French.*
Only then might your hands climb toward
the dizzy molehill of a pressed cotton breast
or encroach down, inch by probative inch,
to that slingshot fork between thighs
that opened, then closed, uncertain,
until she managed *red,* to no one's real
surprise, and the law said you must stop.

Pausing there, hope waiting to pop
like a clutch, your blood's idle revving
and impatient, it was impossible to believe
you would ever actually want to proceed
with caution. So far the drive seemed to need
two, and two lights only, and you were sure
if you knew the road your life would take well
enough and timed its intersections just right
you could make it all the way on nothing but green.

# Cherry Thieves

We were a ravenous pack of wilding
boys on a tear that summer, stripping cherries
from our neighbors' lavishly laden trees,

never asking permission. *Fruit Spree,*
we called it, and *copping cherries,* too young
to know how we were already starting to rob

truth with euphemisms and bits of metaphor,
how we were able to make our theft seem petty,
almost pretty and free of guilt.

The way in a few years we would in lockers,
snapping towels and fibbing to pals
about what we had filched from a girl

the night before in the back seat of the family
Chevy. We had no real sense
of what it would mean to gain this goal

we so blindly sought, could not yet grasp
that having it or not would lie like a mapped line
between the two neighboring states of Paradise

and Lost, nor how a place could shift so quickly
from the one we were in such a hurry
to get to, to the one we wished

we had never been. That summer,
perhaps it was a boy's instinct for practice—
the fledgling's need to master his future part—

that led us without guilt to covet what belonged
to our neighbors, to sneak into each fenced-in garden,
snake up trunks to fruit-bent branches, our mouths

stained and drunk with trespass, preparing
to whisper to a girl when Time turned fortuitous
and cherry-ripe: *Give, give,*

*and I will make you a god.*

# Waste Management

*A beautiful bunch, a ripe banana*
*(Daylight come and me wan' go home)*
*Hide the deadly, black tarantula*
*(Daylight come and me wan' go home)*
—The Banana Boat Song

Trash day, and just now Waste Management
has lumbered through light rain like a mechanical beast
down our tidy cul-de-sac, its two-man crew picking
up a week's worth of garbage, heaving bright orange
city bags into the hungry maw of their panting truck
that seems to snort and paw at the puddled blacktop.
Watching the duo work in tandem to rid

our lives of chaff, I think of Hoffa, of Jersey Mob
jokes, hit jobs topped off with a casket of concrete,
deep-sixed, the perfect mix needed for Cold Cases.
All of that way off, in a far different country, having
little to do with existence here, in our happy little town,
so isolated a postcard popular with tourists claims
we lie two miles beyond The End of the World.

Back where my world began—Kansas City—
muscled black men in tattered overalls would heft
battered bins of un-bagged reek into trucks as flies
swarmed about them in 1950s summer heat.
*Garbage Man!* we'd scream to our little scrum
of pals when we'd hear the grinding gears, the weekly
clamor of galvanized cans invade our neighborhood.

Riding our bikes alongside them for a while—
the closest we could hope to come to Harry Belafonte
on all-white Tracy Street—we'd taunt them with song:
*Day-O…Day-Ay-Ay-O.* Mostly they ignored us.
All we wanted was for one of them to pause, break
character, dare meet our curious stares, sing back:
*Daylight come and me wan' go home.* Even when

we'd fix them in the sights of our Roy Rogers cap
pistols and snap off a few rounds, they'd refuse, stick
to their work, and we'd lose interest, barely watching
as they shoe-laced their way up our newly sanitized street
and vanished. As we would, soon enough, pell-mell
into a future filled with our own tally men, our own weary
backs, our own black tarantulas of diminishment and fear.

Last night on the news: clogged city streets, animated mobs.
Chants of *Hands up, don't shoot.* Phalanx of edgy, armored
troops. And that unmistakable stench of managed waste.

# Taking No Prisoners

Tonight, sleepless, *Sands of Iwo Jima*
on the late movie, I recall our olive-green
and camouflage summers, Army Surplus Store
mean: helmets, bayonet-tipped rifles, ammo
belts, canteens. Summer days we'd establish
our perimeter around the vacant lot, you giving orders
in your best Van Heflin voice: *Take no prisoners!*

Weekends at the Southtown Theater
we'd slog through German snow or French mud
or storm beaches on Pacific islands, learning
little lessons about death, honor, love
of country, duty, the buddy system, about never
relaxing for a smoke when a sniper's bullet
might just as easily have your name on it.

At twenty-two, back from the Marines,
full of *esprit* and *Semper Fi,* you were fit
for nothing but trouble. When you died
I cursed your badly planned retreat:
jobless, in debt, drunk, your used
Cadillac left running behind closed
doors, you, who knew more about engines
than the workings of your low mileage
lemon life. Good soldier, you bore
your secrets to the commandeering flame,
taking no prisoners, leaving nothing
for us to interrogate but a vase
full of ashes, no one to torture
for truth's higher claims, you coward,
you traitor, you sniper's easy prey.

# The Telemachus Gene

*This is my son, mine own Telemachus,*
*To whom I leave the sceptre and the isle, —*
*...Most blameless is he, centred in the sphere*
*Of common duties, ... He works his work, I mine*
—Tennyson, "Ulysses"

Bright sunlight pries you open with its jaws
of life: Time to confront the monster

of another day, one even mere functionary
sons must slay, for that's the script encrypted in your genes.

Nightlong winds have shaken the house, scattered dreams
like bits of torn paper. Nothing remains but abstract

pits of longing and legs weary from dragging the ball
and chain of your father—so many years gone, missing—

through one dreamscape after another. His death: less
peaceful than the blind seer predicted in the oldest existing

version of the story. Each time it's told, yours is never more
than a small, supporting part. On your walk homeward at dusk

through grit-blown streets, every beggar you meet
seems to whisper your name. The bow you could never string

gathers dust in the hall closet. The loom your mother used
to weave her deceit? Long since gone to consignment.

You, sole son and survivor, daily don the mask of hero
with zero for a face. At breakfast, your egg on toast goads you,

baleful as the Cyclop's eye. Like it or not, your story lacks
sweep and scope. Told far from rapt audiences, royal courts,

it unfolds not in smooth meters and polished tropes
but flaccid hexameters, sung by nameless rhapsodes to bone-
    whittled

shades in ragged clothes. Warmed by rotgut and trashcan fires,
they listen: fathers, sons, unholy ghosts.

# My Father's Hands

My father's hands, both of them, lacked
fingertips and nails. The fingers were elliptic,
pink, and smooth, no telltale prints
for him to leave as clues at crime scenes
for prying forensic eyes. I used to lie
awake nights and try to imagine the moment:
his hands, masculine and whole, holding
the dynamite caps out an open window to show
his friends below. Those hands,
about to explode and leave him exposed
mimosa-like to the world, unable to learn
the simplest alphabet of touch, unable to play
a game of catch with his sons. Is that why
he turned to tools, the feel of cold, hard,
unreciprocating steel, the pliant, undemanding
attitude of wood? How often I tracked him
down to his basement shop and saw his tapered
stumps bleeding, his eyes fierce slits through squall
clouds of cigarette smoke, his lathe
raving like a crazed evangelist coercing
miracles from crippled and knotted planks
of pine. When the stroke routed language
from his brain, we could always find him
on trips to Wal-mart pacing the aisles in Tools,
his pared fingers in silent conversation
with sets of chisels and drill bits and clamps.
In his casket, no longer able to hide with sleights
of hand his scarred fingers now dovetailed together,
he smiled. That smile, wired and screwed
into place, bore the slightest trace of pride.
As if, like Noah, he rode the rising waters of his death
in a fine ark of his own making, all gopher wood
and sealed with the purest pitch of darkness.

# So This Is Sex

One warm fall day at recess,
in the shade pool of a weeping willow
near the playground's edge, an older boy,
a seventh grader, told us about it,
like an elder about to reveal the secrets
of the tribe: how the night before,
in a bowered nook, he lay naked
waist-down with a girl, having stripped
in haste, their blue jeans and underwear
tangled about their feet like tethers,
like the tattered husk of childhood.
How, having forced his way in,
he had stopped and withdrew,
guilty perhaps, or afraid he had arrived
too soon at the place boys are schooled
to dream of. *I spilled my seed*
*upon the ground,* he told us,
his language formal and strange.
A few years later when I chanced upon
Onan and Er and a murderous God
in my *King James,* I braked hard mid-verse
at the older boy's exact words.

Even then, the years
at Troost Elementary—pencil bags
and paint pans and practice in cursive
in Big Chief tablets—had already begun
to seem biblical, something I sensed
at the time but could not express,
and would not for many pages
further into my own version

of the saga. But that day, in the shade
of the willow, I am held captive
by one burning image: the sudden spurt
of seed from a slit gunnysack of feed
my grandma pours for her chickens
into an old, dented tin pail.

In Chorus after recess, my changing
voice wrestling with the baritone part
I've been assigned as our class practices
*America the Beautiful,* my only thought:
*So this is sex.* And deep inside my body
I feel endless amber waves of grain
stirring beneath skies spacious
and blue, waiting, patiently
waiting for the thresher's flail.

# Oh, John Wayne

> *I don't feel we did wrong in taking this great country away... Our so-called stealing of [it] from them was just a matter of survival. There were great numbers of people who needed new land, and the Indians were selfishly trying to keep it for themselves.*
>
> —John Wayne, in a *Playboy* interview

Oh, John Wayne, tonight you take me
away to yesteryear. Here you are
on late night cable, in *Rio Grande,*
and I am once more tipping my cavalry
cap to Mother as I head out the door,

my Red Ryder B-B Gun slung over
one shoulder. To our hardened little gang
of Yankee soldiers gathered in the vacant lot,
the only good Apache was a dead one.
To that end we made the barrels

of our Winchesters hotter than Hades
to touch as pagan bands raced bareback
into our deadly fusillade, constantly falling
from their ponies in wild, acrobatic displays,
their painted faces adorning the Texas

prairie of our fervid imaginations. The game
decreed we must be outnumbered.
Thus when afternoon heat pinned us down,
we retreated to the cooling shade
of a tall willow to count our bullets,

calculate our chances. For those pierced
through by arrows, we pretended to snap
off the heads and cauterized wounds
with the red-hot blades of Bowie knives
while Kool-Aid dripped like cheap rye

whiskey down our dusty chins.
Then we waited for reinforcements
to save our Yankee scalps again.
Oh, John Wayne, late the hour, The End near,
credits about to unfurl like Old Glory. Gone

over thirty years, you've left the rest
of us here surrounded and dying
to make a run for it. Most days dawn
with smoke, their signal clear
as the one you saw when cancer's arrow

buried deep in your gut. The cavalry failed
to appear, so you called for a priest,
converted, asked your grave be marked
with an epitaph in Spanish: *Feo, Fuerte*
*y Formal*—Ugly, Strong, Dignified.

Tonight I think of you, Pilgrim, bivouacked
where The West ended, scouting day
and night the Pacific's vast blue, at peace
now, all that land behind you back East
long since parceled, platted, pacified.

# Dailies

*The best film is all the dailies.*
—Federico Fellini

*The reason for the dailies is to sit these people down*
*so they can say This is what I did yesterday.*
—Robert Altman

Oh, you know it is there somewhere, a life
good enough for the dark theater, good enough
for the little speech you carry folded in your pocket,
a speech modest and full of itemized gratitudes.

But each morning when you sit down to review
the day's previous shoot, you find nothing in the takes,
not a single true gesture or scene or close-up, not even
a solid establishing shot. As for tone, style, mood,

even here you hesitate. Sure, you know the options—
*noire, vérité, montage*, etc. And you know
the greatest directors deftly convert such clichés
into cinematic gold. Your problem?

How to translate this singular life to the Big Screen,
make it work, give it the art it has always deserved
along with real box office appeal. Meanwhile cast
and crew grow restless. The silent hours mill about

like extras hoping for a speaking part. The lead actress,
with whom you sleep, is already dreaming
of new projects. Your dog keeps pissing at the foot
of your director's chair and will no longer bark on cue.

The Best Boy has twice run off with the Grip.
Your producer parents died years ago. The critics,
your children, view your long delayed debut as just
another inexcusable failure. And location? Change

it now? Unthinkable. But each day the cameras
barely begin to roll when you hear yourself
screaming *Cut! Cut!* The light is still wrong.
So is the darkness. You must try it again.

# Home Movies

I drive my mother through the old
neighborhood, my mother of the fractured
hip, bent spirit so lacking calcium
it is stooped and splintered. She winces
at the demographic changes time
has brought. The past is that other
country, the one for which her passport
has expired. *There,* she tells me, pointing
to a boarded window. Right there,
in a chair, is where she nursed both
of her sons. I was the one, she says,
who fussed, who never got enough,
and I feel in her voice the stropped
edge of something she has never quite been able
to leave behind. I can still link all
the houses with names from top
to bottom of our block, still retrieve
faces and moments for each, like scenes
cropped and left on the cutting room floor.
This whole week of my visit, we've talked
in her dark and airless apartment
of the gone days on Tracy Street, playing
them over in words like old home movies
all in black and white and so dubbed
over and over again in memory,
principal players rendered so unfamiliar
by death that the footage seems out
of focus and strange. So, like prisoners
stumbling outside of Plato's cave, we drive
around the block once more and slow
again in front of the house that recurs

to me in dreams. A tall angular boy sits
on the front steps, a basketball turning on
one stiff finger like a newly discovered planet.
*Stop!* she tells me. She stares hard
at the boy, as if his blackness were a prop
badly placed, the house, perhaps all the world
itself, an unbelievable stage, an elaborate
trick of the eye. This will be her last
take. She wants to get it right.

# Revenge

From the time you were just a kid, pimpled
and skinny and riddled with BBs
from your older brother's constant snipings
you feasted on Charles Atlas ads
in magazines, the ones where geeks
like you got sand kicked in their faces
before they got wise on Dynamic Tension,
beefed up, and scared the kicker shitless in the end.
But wishing had no power to conceal the scent
of your fear, and bullies tracked you like packs
of feral dogs. You could almost bear high school
English when Montagues slew Capulets, or vice versa,
and Hamlet spent the last scene mopping up the stage.
Friday nights at the neighborhood theater
when John Wayne settled long overdue accounts
with Japs and Apaches, you could walk a little
taller on the jittery trek home, and sleep came easier
by half when the Caped Kryptonian sped faster
than a bullet through your dreams and heroes
decked out like bats or made of plastic
kept order on the city's Manichean streets.

Now, despite years of Corleones and Clint Eastwoods,
of Stallones and avenging cyborgian angels,
the grim contest seems to grow more and more
one-sided. You've lost track of the score.
You used to count yourself among the bleeding
hearts, full of nothing but sweetness
and light, but deep down you've begun to long
for your hamstrung country to kick a little ass,
and you would sleep much better with a gun
if only your wife would let you have one.

So you keep a loaded bat, a cracked Louisville Slugger,
propped behind your bedroom door, and you nap
like a Looney Tunes hound, one eye open,
ears trained like the crosshairs of an infrared scope
on the dark's smatter of small alarming sounds.
Most nights it's a hard ride to the borderland of sleep,
but once there, it's your kind of country,
and you could track a flea through the whole
freakin' Badlands if you had to. When you finally catch
up to the world, it freezes. *Where do you want it?*
you ask. *The Belly? The Back?* It's your turn now.
You point your pearl-handled cannons
at its jackbooted feet. *Dance,* you say. Its spurs
percuss the dust like stricken tambourines.
*Dance!* you say again. *Faster.*

# The Drinker

No one could ever explain to him
the meaning of enough. Evenings
he would come to us down the sidewalk
from the city, from the work he hated
to love, a bottle in brown paper
from Lafferty's Liquors gripped
in one hand, his thumb tucked beneath
the fingers of the other as if it were
some small final thing to hold onto.

Conversations of ice in a glass
of bourbon were more familiar now
to us than his voice, which he left
mostly at the office or saved
for fighting late at night with Mother,
who long since had moved sex
and other silken things out of their room.

His talent and art were the drinker's:
He knew how to slip a thin reed deep
into the dark secret earth to sip
from its coolest pooled spaces,
or kneel to suck sweet droplets
from a tuber when what would slake
his thirst had vanished from its normal
singing places. No mortal's thirst
moved him. Only divinity perhaps
could fathom such need, could rise
for work each morning at five,
unencumbered, while what he had made
from his breath and blood and seed
lay dry and wasted all about him.

Only divinity could lie and dissemble,
seeing always beyond a world's immediate
pangs and cries of defeat to the millennium
when no possible thirst would go unappeased.

For this reason, that July of great drought,
record heat, when fish leapt from Missouri's
scalding streams for relief and the city's
stinking airless rooms and alleys betrayed
their aged and impoverished dead like a dream
of apocalyptic plague, we jabbed
his cold body into the parched earth.
For this reason, we returned that evening,
climbing the tall cemetery fence at dusk
to rain whiskey on his grave's cracked lips,
just to say with hearts dehydrated
by grief: *Father, Father,*

*forgive.*

# Hamlet: A Revision

Let's say Act V did not end with you
taking the poisoned foil deep in the gut.
You might have been able to keep on
reading philosophy late into the night,
you might have found someone
to settle down with, someone to bear
your overly sensitive children, someone
who would have put up with those antic
dispositions you so liked to feign.
And what then? Would your chronic doubts
have receded in old age, or would you
still be stabbing at every arras that fluttered,
trying to connect the world out there
with the one inside your head?
Would you have kept on conversing
late at night on torch-lit towers
with the dead, chatting with apparitions
even after truth had proven itself
beyond the merest shadow of a doubt?

When your high-strung children,
querulous and at wit's end, moved you
to that home for passive aggressive princes,
would you have continued to suffer
the platitudes of garrulous old men
once your place at their table had been set?
Would you still insist on consorting
with fools to relieve your tacit fear of death,
crave the company of gravediggers for the comic
relief last acts so often seem to require?
That framed likeness on the nightstand

by your bed? Admit it. You still want
her, the mother you ruthlessly stabbed
with daggered words, the mother critics said
you'd go to your grave wishing you never had.

# The Runaway

*—After a painting by Norman Rockwell*

In the restaurant, a man excuses himself
        from his wife, his friends, his rack
of lamb, the drinks that have finally begun
        to plane smooth the day's splintered edges.
In the lavatory, while his lame, diminished
        stream delays its advent, he stares as he has
for years at the framed print hanging
        above the urinal. How many times,
the man wonders, has he pissed brooding
        beneath this same picture? Recalling
its steadfast presence through the deaths
        of two friends, the near collapse of his marriage,
the slow-to-heal estrangement of one
        of three children, he knows this simple
framed image has been one of the few constants
        in a score of persistently shifting years.
He knew whose painting it was
        and he also knew he was not supposed
to like it. Such sentimental looking back
        to a past mostly mythologized, such a varnished
view of America: this is what so galled true
        connoisseurs of beauty. But he was moved
nevertheless, as if a neurosurgeon's probe
        had stumbled upon some uncharted declivity
in his brain, one that contained all his pleasures,
        real or imagined, from childhood.
Now, looking again at the picture's fixed
        moment, the man feels at once both exiled
from and pulled into the story: a towheaded boy
        and a cop sitting together in a diner,
talking, while the cook behind the counter
        leans close, smiling, listening to what

the boy and cop have to say. At the boy's feet,
        what little a runaway needs wrapped in a red
bandanna and tied to a stick. The narrative
        line, the man guesses, is supposed to be clear,
reassuring, but it leaves him feeling vaguely unsettled.
        Most of his life he has dreamed
about running. From family, from friends,
        from the angina-like press of routine
that often wakes him at night and leaves him
        frightened and barely able to breathe.
There in the dark he wonders what of value
        he might fit into a bindle. What destination
would set him free from his own querulous
        soliloquies, his mind's non-stop interrogations?
As a child he had come to the end of books
        that made him want to fade away
from his own constrained life and enter
        plots he knew must continue somewhere after the last
turned page. His bladder empty, he continues
        to stare at the wistful little vignette
in front of him. One voice urges him to go
        back to his wife, his friends, and his now cold
meal, and a second cajoles him to trade places
        with the boy in the painting, to be young again,
to ride his thumb toward every selfish whim.
        But a third, the one he knows best, asks
the kinds of questions that freeze a failed Romantic
        like him in his tracks, as if he himself
were nothing but a static image captured in paint
        as he stands before this urinal. Would the wedge
of apple pie that must lie on the counter in front
        of the boy taste sweet or bitter? Would the glass

of milk before him be half full and cold, or warm
    and half empty? Would the cop's eyes be distilled
with kindness or shifting and distant?
    Who but himself will miss him if he chooses
to run away? Who but himself will love
    him if he decides to stay?

# *Ex Post Facto*: Rhetoric 101

*We make out of the quarrel with others, rhetoric, but of the quarrel with ourselves, poetry.*
—William Butler Yeats, "Anima Hominis," *Essays*

From such distance, I can't remember much
of that day except the heat—Missouri,
mid-summer—your face—earnest, insistent,

black as a polished boot—and what
you said when you stopped me in the hall
after class: That I was, by virtue of being white,

a racist. *Inescapable,* you added, the word falling hard
like a gavel. Because the goal of the course was writing
sound arguments, I might have asked

you to turn a more careful eye on your logic,
or to recall our week's work on enthymemes,
how risk often lurks in an unstated premise.

But you rarely attended, and when you did,
you sat apart in the back row, aloof, dismissive,
a supercilious smile scribbled across your face.

New enough to teaching to be flummoxed,
I struggled to rebut your unsupported claim,
all the while inwardly fuming: *Have you no sense*

*of caution in dealing with your teacher?*
*Who are you to betray me like this*
*in front of my many contradictory selves?*

*And why do I persist in playing Peter*
*to your Judas with my repeated, heated denials?*
You parried my objections with that vexing grin.

Then, like a shrewd prosecutor suddenly resting
his case, you spun on your heels and vanished,
first into the hall's steady stream of students,

and then from the course itself,
never bothering to drop. From the standpoint
of rhetoric, a clever tactic, setting me up

like that to lose. At term's end I argued with you
in your absence about your grade before I made you
pay. In my head I heard you say, *Drink*

*for the rest of your days from this well*
*into which I have poured my poison.* I do.
This poem is a quarrel with myself, not you,

who deserved an A.

# Whatever The Darkness Brings

*The art of dying begins with preparation.*
—The Tibetan Book of the Dead

For days I've kept you at bay with wind
and blowing snow and ashen light and rote
routine. But nights, when my lamp gives way
to dark, it crumbles, this frail firewall I've labored
to build between me and thoughts that hammer
each other like polished steel balls
in a Newton's Cradle.

On cue you come,
unfleshed spirit now, holographic stunt,
memory's wraith. You, whose sudden exit
in sleep last week capsized loved ones in rapids
of disbelief. For years we waded rivers, drifted
lakes, fishing as night sifted down and stars began
to dimple the surface of the sky. Our talk stayed
mostly shallow, but it would deepen those times
someone close to us, kith or kin, had withered
slowly, then vanished. Much like boys pressing
freshly pricked fingers together, bound forever
by blood, we swore: Whatever the darkness
brings, should luck allow us to see it
coming, we would cheat, pull the rug plumb out
from under Death, steal its thunder
with stockpiled pills or one of the shotguns
you used each fall for hunting pheasants.
Grief, we agreed, was for the living
to bear. We'd be out of it. Unencumbered
by the body's coarse cloth, we'd take our boxed
seats in sweet oblivion. *Out of it*: That's what
we called it those nights fat browns battened
on the evening hatch and we passed a small jar

of good scotch back and forth, both of us then
still very much at home in the cozy garb
of modest and pleasant lives. No shilly-
shallying around, we promised. No *Mother*
*May I* baby steps, no pussy-footing toward
that platitude, the grave.

Maybe you did see
it coming. The rest of us lacked such luck.
Your death arrived like a test, unannounced
and final. Cheating begets cheaters, so our eyes
dart about in the dark, roving for answers.
Anything would do—scribbled snippets
of nonsense, a few cribbed phrases.
Anything to silence this totally blank page.

*—for Jerry Udesen: Brother-In-Law, River Keeper*

# Those Who Can, Do

*Be one upon whom nothing is lost:*
This bit of Henry James just one
of the many small pills of wisdom
I dispensed to students for too many years.
*Wake up!* I shouted, striking
my desk, assuring them Thoreau
would have done likewise were he there
to lend visual force to his wish
that they stop snoozing their lives away.
Term after term I warned them
*ad nauseam* how in poems rain and wind
are seldom simple scenic bits of weather
for verisimilitude's sake, that they are visible
signs of the indiscernible, workings of mystery
and grace on souls in need of breath and drink.
Why then have I dozed all morning over
a blank page, as mired as the Ancient Mariner
upon his painted ocean, dull as the brain
of the poet himself, crippled by opium,
while a summer Lake Superior rain spatters
my window and a vast wind fills the maples' sails,
the house strains at its moorings,
and I, so at ease sailing the shimmering seas
of others, have no strength to free
my lines and cast off from this dock?

# Boating To The Dreamland Bar And Grill

*Surely, surely, slumber is more sweet than toil...*
—Tennyson, "The Lotos-Eaters"

You steer for land, just as Ulysses did
in that other myth right before his men, grown tired,
found themselves seduced by dreams of escape.
No one needs to remind you of the many points
at which your story and his diverge.
Ulysses refused, and the only lotus blossoms here
will be a few beers and a plate of fried fish.
Nor is your estranged wife devoted and waiting
at home, weaving shrouds to buy you more time.
If there are suitors in her life, you would be the last
to know, and even if you did, you can't remember
the last time you strung an arrow in your bow.
Why is it a place for dreams, this bar and grill
so far out on the Bootjack Road it's better reached
by boat? Rumor has it during the days of boom
copper it was a hotel with a fleet of prostitutes.
On paydays one could rise up from his labors
deep in the earth to buy himself a cheap binge
and a quickie or two—about as far as dreams went
for the Finns and other immigrant moles
who made their mine bosses rich enough to leave
them all behind in toxic piles of tailings
and chemical spills. Bent over your meal, you dream,
but not from the food or the slow-motion waitress.
And the locals at the bar—loggers, odd-jobbers—
are certainly not speaking in languid whispers.

At the Dreamland dock you sit in your boat
sipping another beer, waiting for the festering sun,
blind and bloody as the Cyclops' eye,
to disappear. The homeward journey

will take minutes rather than years. You need
no assistance from a blind prophet.
That aureole of light in the distance?
Not the beckoning fires of Ithaca,
but Houghton's bare, denotative glare.
You know perfectly well these Portage waters,
so placid tonight, can swiftly rise to a torn bag
of ill winds and blow you far off course.
You've been there before, and had more than your fill
of enchanted women. For years you felt fear
a siren's song at midnight could instill,
but you no longer think very hard about death.
As the gods will, a boat becomes a raft,
a raft a spar, and there's nothing left but to swim,
putting one hand in front of the other, digging
deep into that element in which your life began.

# The Rehearsal

*Marco!* the boy shouts, eyes pressed shut
as he stumbles in water nearly over his head.
*Polo!* the man replies, as he must
because the game requires it.
Playing with his son in the hotel
pool and trying to evade his own hounding
brain, the man recalls reading in college
that children's games are dress rehearsals
for their own far off deaths. He had scoffed
then but it seems true enough now:
death's blindness, its unrelenting pursuit,
the way it makes up the rules as it goes
and taps this or that fleeing shoulder
or toe almost by accident. Yesterday,
he sat half dozing on the beach in the shade
of a palm tree, nagged by envy
as he watched a young couple caress
and press against one another in the Gulf
of Mexico surf. One moment, this tan,
muscled youth seemed a perfect icon
of desire as he dove into the translucent
green crescendo of a wave, the next
mute witness to caprice as he returned
to land by chopper in a body bag.
The man thought of all those childhood
dusks of Hide & Seek, Tag, Blind Man's
Bluff, of his own parents vanished, the growing
list of others taken, ready or not.
*Marco!* screams his son again, closing
fast, his lips blue, his face ecstatic,
but before the man can reply or twist
away he feels a chilled hand slap
against his sunburned back. *You're it!*

the boy shrieks, delighted. And the man
is, and he knows it. And before he takes
his turn, before he closes his eyes to begin
the chase, he grabs his son and holds
him, holds on for this dearest of lives.

# Seizing The Day

This morning, before our son flew back
to his job in Phoenix, he showed us
a tattoo he'd kept hidden, a blue
arabesque of lines and signs meaning,
he told us, *Carpe Diem,* the one
single thing he could think to do, he said,
when a close friend took his own life
for no good reason. You know,
he explained, *Eat, drink, make merry...*
as if his pain had earned him the right
now to be our teacher, as if his mother
and I had never before tried to curl
fetal around the present moment,
never done our best to forget
that one good morrow or another
we must die. I wanted to say something
wise, warn him about theatrics
yet to come. But a father is without
wisdom in his son's country, and life
prefers showing over telling,
so I said nothing but a hug.

Now it's late afternoon. As the light
fades, I prepare dinner that once
again has dwindled to the two of us.
We listen to the evening news:
the economy still trying to make up
its mind, the Dow once more amped
like a junkie on a pogo stick.
Lost jobs, lost homes, lost savings.
At my cutting board, with its medley
of citrus and fresh herbs,
the news still coming at us
ready or not, I decide to try it

again, living just in the present
moment. One at a time I lift
pressed garlic, fresh basil, a slice
of lime to my face, breathing each in,
and for a minced instant past
and future vanish: the former,
where Death reigns supreme,
the latter, where Death lies
patiently in wait. For a heart beat
or two I am absent from thought
before this dollop of day I've seized
by the throat thrashes and kicks,
breaking my white-knuckled hold.

# A Picture's Worth A Thousand Words

Who, I find myself wondering this late afternoon
   as I look out my window at lazy traces of snow,
who first captured this timeless adage in the web

of words, and with such pith, given the spendthrift nature
   of language? A Chinese proverb perhaps,
some ancient snippet of Confucian wisdom.

Or that master of stillness Basho, whose frugal snapshots
   of moons and clouds, of ponds and frogs and silence,
all in three lines and seventeen taut syllables,

still leave us with a nifty balance of nine hundred and eighty
   plus pennies in our stuffed piggybank of words.
But my browser reveals the ordinary: A 1913 newspaper

ad for an auto supply house in Piqua, Ohio—
   *One look at our endless inventory is worth*
*a thousand words.* I imagine myself in the bitter

cold at 133 North Main, in downtown Piqua,
   nose pressed to the store window's glass,
that 24/7 voice in my head rendered momentarily mute

as I stare at shelf after shelf of neatly labeled parts,
   row upon row of jet black tires glistening in their stacked racks.
Planted there, transfixed, I'm a perfect simulacrum

of antiquated desire. A verb-less picture. Jump
   cut: This morning, walking the dog in fresh snow
near campus in the rutted alley back of fraternity row,

I happen upon Barbie, naked, lashed to a tree, her hands
tied behind her, a half-spent firework jammed
between her once-creamy thighs. Her mascaraed eyes

still distant, dreamy. Immune to surprise.

## Retreat

Alone at their cabin, in retreat
        from a life bleeding
                and unstaunched, he stands

at the stove trying to remember
        how much of each his wife would
                boil—water and sugar—

and how long before she would turn
        water into wine with a squeeze
                from the vial of red food

coloring. In his mind he could see her lift
        the glass globe like a chalice to its hook
                above the porch window,

calling the hummers back, as if her body,
        her blood itself were the sacrifice,
                freely offered. And always

they returned, drumming the air,
        blurring all day from leafy
                shadows to levitate or perch

in their greed, in their search
        for an end to simple hungers.
                They would drink until the generous

cup was empty, until, she liked to say,
        you'd think they would faint,
                or burst. At the stove, still

lingering and confused, he wonders:
        Is this how it was in the beginning?
                Might it be so again at the last

luminous place? No vying
        in the ceaseless soporific beating
                of wings. Quietude.

Guileless mouths asleep on
        the sweet, world-without-end
                nipple of a generous god.

# Our World

*A shudder in the loins engendered there*
*The broken wall, the burning roof and tower*
*And Agamemnon dead.*
—W. B. Yeats, "Leda and the Swan"

You read about the boy killing swans
in the *Our World* section of the evening paper
and try to understand it. You can almost see him,
naked, gliding toward that silhouette of island,
his path marked only by his wake, a widening V
through the pond's moonlit stillness. You hear
the dares and jeers of his friends as they stand
drinking beer by the small fire on the beach.
And perhaps because you have been duped
by poets to believe the rape of Leda by Zeus
produced Helen's immortal beauty, even now,
half way into this bit of filler story, you still want
to believe good can be kin to the ugly and bad.

But this is our world, where meaning is a game
of shells, the boy nothing more than a drunk
college student who tricked two cygnets with bits
of biscuit, kicked them to death, stunned
the mother with a rock, then hacked off her head
with the small dull blade of his pocket knife.
Next, as if jumbled fragments of ancient myth
yet tumbled in his blood, he sodomized her
and swam back to the beach, her severed nape
caught gently like a trophy between his teeth.
Nothing engendered there on that treeless island—
no broken wall, no burning tower of Troy,
no Agamemnon dead. Just an ice pick of rage,
chipping at the frozen sea of your heart,
and the best you can do is turn the page.

# Dream Girl

*The girl of my dreams is the sweetest girl of all the girls I know...*
—lyric from *The Sweetheart of Sigma Chi*

*The blue of her eyes, the gold of her hair,* Oh yes,
we could each see her in our future, though it was still
for the most part an unmapped continent. Once a month
after dinner, dressed in coat and tie, we would move
to the sun room with our House Mother for coffee,
and with our demitasse cups and saucers we would gather
around the piano to practice the song the movies had made
famous. Each time one of us gave his little jeweled pin
to his girl we would send a dozen white roses,
and later, studies ended for the night, we walked as one
to the girl's sorority for our Candlelight Ritual.
We stood quietly for a time beneath her window
before our voices, one hundred strong, would join
in that familiar song, our dreamy La Tour faces limned
in the candles' pale glow, faces on which so little
had yet been written.

We could not then dream
of a time when the flawless pedestaled girls
would step down and become women haunted
by neglect, post partum blues, varicose veins,
adipose tissue. Nor could we dream how many of us
would slip and slide up the greased skids of work
or slowly drift from our families into booze and failed
quests for memory's perfect sweethearts.
How the women behind our eyes in sleep—the few
we had truly wanted, the ones we carelessly threw
away—would come back to make us ache with sex
and other hungers before they startled us awake
with their merciless goodbyes. How we would lie

in the dark and assay the overworked and thinning
ore of our lives, creep closer to the turned backs,
the heat, the unapproachable mystery of our wives,
and whisper: *Stay. Stay.*

# Hurricane Season

Footage on the morning news shows red flags stabbing
inland, snapping out terse alerts along the Gulf coast

all the way to Texas. A Category 4 battens offshore,
its unblinking, insatiable eye lazing steadily toward The Keys.

So human, the progress of this seasonal weather:
Mounting depression, circular reasoning winds that counter time,

torrents and tides that flood and recede, leaving mud
to feed memory. One September years ago we woke in Bermuda

to news of Faye's approach. Giddy with youth, we hastened
down to the Flatts to buy what we thought would see us through—

candles, matches, rum, a cheese cake. Palm fronds plunged
in a wind yellow and estranged and blew like the loosened hair

of Maenads in some ancient orgiastic ritual.
All day and far into the night the storm raced straight at us

from south and east. Stay, we vowed. Ride it out. Wait.
Welcome the hardening darkness. So we stayed, gauging

tides and knotted wind, tracing by radio her certain coming,
hoping to trade her eye for eye. Near midnight, just forty miles

out from that reef-guarded hook of island, she veered north.
We lit candles and raised our glasses to the tempest we had missed.

Much later, when it finally hit, the one we had so patiently tracked
for years, it took us with no warning and little surprise,

and no roads left open to higher, safer ground.

*—for D. G.*

# Roland Redux

*...neither pride*
*Nor hope rekindling at the end descried,*
*So much as gladness that some end might be.*
—Robert Browning, "Childe Roland to the Dark Tower Came"

You're in it every day, The News: They
tower above. You, small and weak, cower
below. You—who slobber in a slop of mud,
a ruck of snow, whose nose so freely bleeds,
whose clobbered glasses crack—you'd flee
if there were truly anyplace to go except
behind your mother's skirts, which any kid
would know's the very worst, and she is dead
besides, so very long ago.

And even if you clenched your fists,
stood your ground, refused to run, what
exactly could you find to punch? The world's
grown ever more abstract. And if you cast
an ersatz brick, oblivious, they duck
behind their quick-fix vows, allowing facts
to slip with ease from off their slick
and downy backs.

The clapper's cracked; the chapel—locked—
has gone to wrack and ruin. Unfledged
Roland knew it long ago: Nothing left
at eventide but his bequest. So down you go,
riding into darkness that quickly surrounds.
You lift your bunged-up bugle to your lips.
You blow.

# II

# Salvage

*Why? That my chaff might fly; my grain lie, sheer and clear.*
—Gerard Manley Hopkins, "Carrion Comfort"

# Alien Sex

I stood on the porch that night,
the lights from a parent's car just vanishing
at the end of the street. My friend and I
had been to a movie, *It Came From*
*Outer Space.* Above me, the stars
had lost their innocence. My block

throbbed with threats from distant galaxies.
Because I was late, I entered the house
quietly, hoping to sneak unnoticed upstairs.
All seemed normal enough for the usual
Saturday night of too much drinking—
My parents, asleep, he in his chair

in front of the guttering television screen,
she splayed out on the studio couch
in a nearby room. How quickly
the known world can turn strange.
I knew what it was when I saw it
on the living room floor. I had swiped

them from Crown Drugs and filled them
with water to ambush passing cars. This one,
viscous, lay damply coiled on the rug
like the sloughed husk of a newborn alien
that must have streaked from deepest space
even as my friend and I hunkered down

in the Southtown Theater's three-dimensional
darkness. My brain, agitated,
could come to only two conclusions,
one so fantastic my mind refused
the gross picture it posed. The only credible
way to explain it: Extraterrestrials.

Either way, I had no choice but to destroy
the evidence, picking the sticky chrysalis
skin up with a thick wad of Kleenex
and shoving it deep in the kitchen trash
right alongside my own astonishment.
Upstairs, I tried hard to distract myself

with prayer, but that wet rubber
crackled in my mind's air like static
and there was no getting through
that night to the starry kingdom of God.
Next morning at breakfast, I studied them
carefully through my new 3-D glasses,

my father in profile with his coffee
and Sunday paper, Mother a bit
groggy at the stove, tending
pans of bacon and eggs. Nothing
amiss: no telltale scales on his hands,
no saw-toothed tail switching beneath

her gossamer robe. All through breakfast
I stayed vigilant, my eyes as sharp
as Flash Gordon's, my mind hyper
with the ammo of fight or flight.
After breakfast I planned to search
in our backyard for the crater, the mother ship

I knew it would contain.
I would bravely destroy the invaders.
Then it would be my most solemn duty
to inform the world: From now on
here, on Planet Earth, things would never,
ever again be the same.

# Audition

We didn't handle snakes but we were Rock
of Ages hard on sinners, a role we gladly beat
into our fervent breasts each week
until, come Sunday, we could bathe ourselves
buff new in the blood of a sweet and loving Jesus
*who died who died who died,* Reverend Pinkerton preached,
to meet us more than half way to the eternal kingdom.
When I stood and said I had heard the call, I fibbed.
I was nine and wanted the *King James* version,

the Red Letter edition with the Lord's exact words
printed in the color of His own shed blood.
So I lied and found myself standing one Sunday
morning in front of the fat and ruddy muster
of the Rockhill Baptist Church, let Reverend Pinkerton immerse
me in my smock of pure white, then, to claim my *King
James,* I had to recite all six verses of the 23rd Psalm:
the green pastures and still waters, the march
through death's shadowy valley, the comfort of rod

and staff, the lack of fear, the oily head and constantly
spilling cup. It was a poor audition. I made
enough mistakes to see that Bible slipping,
but the grace of water dripping from my chin
so much like a wannabe's tears fooled even me
enough to win the part and make me think,
like David, I had landed myself a place world
without end (or at least for a good run of years)
in the safe standing-room-only house of the Lord.

# Playing With Fire

*The universe... has always been, is, and always will be*
*an ever-living fire.*
—Heraclitus

Who also said, *Time is a game played*
*beautifully by children.* And so it was, always,
with us, even that day in the vacant lot
behind our two houses where we were playing,
not with the usual bat, ball, and carefully-oiled mitt,
but with matches, striking and flinging
them willy-nilly into the dry, whispering grass.
Kids who couldn't see beyond impulse
to what most certainly lay ahead.
If we were young empiricists, hungering
to understand what made our planet stay
spinning so steadily on its axis, we were still
mostly just boys devoted to play. When *Presto!*
fire encircled us in its charmed ring
and, fed by a warm breeze, sped outward,
at first we jumped with unabated joy
like Greeks dancing and drumming
their chests as Troy succumbed to flames.
Then, amazed, we spotted Mrs. McCatty,
ancient and crazed neighbor, wobbling
toward us, clutching in palsied hands
the snarled hose she'd snatched from her garden
and shrieking *Fire!* like some told-you-so
crone of a Cassandra. So we scrapped our epic
pose, swore we heard sirens in the distance,
and bolted home, the onc safe place,
though we knew our mothers would flay us
with knotted words then send us sulking
to our rooms to await the final judgment
of fathers. I can still hear mine stepping

onto the front porch, grateful to have survived
the grinding wheel of another day,
ready for drinks and the evening paper.
Then Mother's grave, muffled news,
Father's weary plod up stairs, the way
Sisyphus must have felt trying to imagine
himself happy. I have no recollection
of what punishment ensued. Now,
after many years of mixed wins and losses,
this I choose to remember: two boys spot-lit
in a vacant lot, trying hard to extinguish
the future, while all around us it burned.

*—for Bill Wakefield*

# Radical Mastectomy

When she first came back
from the surgeon's studio,
you would not let her model
for you what he had undone...
though she would have bared
for you that scarred and carmine
skin with a woman's joy too kin
to madness for a man
ever to touch. In the darkened
gallery of sleep you grieved
each other as a lost winter
glove grieves its missing
armature of hand.

*So this is love,*
you think at last, the night
you lift her soft bandage gown,
your tongue delicate at first
to trace the curved absence,
memory's taste. This string
on your finger, what is it
for? Oh, how your vanished mother
would stand at the door in a sepulcher
of snow so many winter mornings
ago, her trace of a woman's kiss
turned ice on your lips as you ran
to the bus gloveless, her bidding
faint through muffled ears: *Search,*
*make sure you search the Lost and Found.*

# Saving The Movies

Perhaps it's possible after all to believe
in unseen centripetal plans against the random.
Einstein's brain turns up in brine

behind a beer cooler in central Kansas.
And discovered now, deep within
a salt mine where sky and wheat refrain

like a hymn that has no end, the original
*Gone with the Wind,* itself forgotten,
almost lost in the dimming lineage

of prints, copies of copies copied,
colors bleached, sound abstracted, scenes
cropped through use like one wise man

cancelled from a Christmas crèche,
fives or sixes struck from faces
of clocks. Old movies, classics,

sights and sounds of half our century
nearly vanished, now redeemed
by industries of love—that small Promethean

cell helping us rebel against the unsteady
state of things, descending now and then
from the sky like a mechanical god to untie

our badly tangled plots. As if Rhett might turn
back at the film's end to unburn Atlanta,
unsay his famous kiss-off of Scarlett,
and claim there *is* a single damn to give.

# First Dibs

Family and friends are always first—
before Good Will, the Salvation Army—
closets and drawers and bookshelves thrown
open for us to take what suits us, mementos
of the newly dead, and of our own dying
too, although even with squinting hard
we can't really see the latter just yet,
or if we do, we're not quite ready to believe.
A shirt, a sport coat, a class ring, a box of tools
for keeping one's world in a state of constant,
improvised repairs. In our defense:
*Waste not, want not.* And surely the dead
would nod, if they could, in agreement.

But when you died, I couldn't conceive
taking your battered leather satchel,
couldn't imagine it slung over my shoulder
as I headed off to teach. I could not bear
the thought of wearing your favorite tweed
jacket as I stood in front of a class
or sat with friends over drinks. So instead,
I took your wife and two young sons.

*First dibs!* we shouted long ago
when we saw something we wanted
to nab ahead of our pals. Just boys,
trying to school ourselves in the taker's arts
of reflex and greed. I wanted what you loved
most of all, thereby keeping your death
up close and personal. And it still is,
almost thirty years later. Thirty years
since she said she wanted me

to have something of yours. I took
only what I needed, having learned
the hard way by then to moderate my
greed, to keep it within a range my
heart could claim sustainable, or nearly so
in this thread-bare, hand-me-down world.

*—for Bruce*

# Girl At Mirror

*—After A Painting By Norman Rockwell*

The woman had come because her husband wanted
        to kindle memory, to see again the images
he claimed defined him as a boy, images
        that came monthly to his house, resting for weeks
on coffee table and kitchen counter and bathroom
        hamper, images he swore had shaped
his sense of growing up in America.
        She'd studied art in college

and remembered the dismissal and scorn
        her teachers preached for mere illustrations
of The Real. So she had prepared herself
        not to like what people of taste she knew
disdained. Nor did it help that she found,
        in every gallery room, tourists
in striped shirts and white belts and gold chains

        and tight fitting clothes gushing bloated approval
because, for them, every canvas seemed to contain
        a fool's gold nugget of truth imbued with a smile
or a pinch of nostalgic rue, because to them
        beauty meant the world they knew had been reproduced
perfectly in paint. And it was true
        that in the course of an hour the woman found
a great deal to dismiss: rustic rubes

        in antic poses, do-good Boy Scouts and
avuncular barbers and tomboys with black
        eyes and sentimental fêtes for FDR's
*Four Freedoms,* which she believed in
        the cash nexus of America were mostly sham
anyway. But one painting kept her

circling back: A girl in a white lace slip
sitting before a mirror, peering quizzically
at herself, her doll on the floor tipped
over or falling, as if this simple act
of adolescent self-absorption meant time
for childhood play had suddenly passed.
At her feet an opened lipstick, a comb, a box
of powdered rouge. On her lap a magazine,
open to a photo of a Hollywood star

whose glamour seemed impossibly far removed
from what the girl saw returning her gaze
in the mirror: Those wistful eyes that said
she had glimpsed something of the transient
nature of beauty, the consequences of time.
The woman recognized the allusive nod
the canvas made to old masters, (Velazquez,

LaTour) whose pensive women gazing
into mirrors documented in paint the very dawning
of self-consciousness. And because she knew
a painting, no matter how abstract,
invites its viewers to step inside the frame,
to make the implied story theirs with footage
from their own lives, it was now she
staring into that mirror, remembering

how once she, too, in her ugly phase felt farther away
than ever from the swan her parents promised.
How the inaudible whisper of longing
had grown into a moan for which she could find
no voice. When she was twelve, she had sat
just like this one night, gazing into the mirror

of her vanity, just hours after the blood prophesied
by her mother had begun to seep from
between her thighs while she sat at a movie
with friends. And she remembered how
a few weeks later, and without her even knowing
it, she found her thoughts orbiting around a boy
she'd never really noticed, a boy who suddenly
burned in the night sky of her mind
like a bright and newly discovered planet.

She remembered how his first tight-lipped kiss
made her want both less and more. How is it possible,
she recalled thinking then—a question that bothers
her still—to know wrong from right
when both flesh and spirit extemporize
in such eloquent, deceptive tongues?
She is startled to feel the hand of her husband, soft,

stabilizing, on her shoulder, calling her back.
The hand she had seized at first to keep
her from falling, the hand that had led her
through the loss of their first child, the one that helped
her unravel the hopeless mare's nest of a placebo
lover, the one a few years later still willing
to worship in the ruined temple of a vanished breast.
Hand in hand they browsed the gift shop,

then made their way down the winding path
to the parking lot. It was early
October, and the Berkshires were in full scale
revolt against the looming absence of color.
On the drive home, they stopped at a stand
for pumpkins, and as they carried the one
they'd chosen to their car, something about

the slant of the dying sun, the burning hills,
        and the autumnal drumming of her heart
led her to wonder how long life might otherwise
        have seemed, and art longer still, were we not so
much like foolish painters asleep at our easels,
        sure that beauty would patiently hold its pose
and the morning light remain forever.

# Retired From Television, The Sex Therapist Explains

*—Sarasota, Florida*

They say so nearly perfect is the human ear
it can almost hear as background
noise molecules collide, and soon
enough I began to hear them:
the ones who would never call—
Lenny in LA or Deborah far away in Kansas
riding in silence the body's long
slow earthward glide.

Those out there
who would never reveal the touch
of strangers or dreams of proletariat
hands, the ones sleeping in separate
rooms and hearing the faint first
whispers of their own histories.
The ones who would never call to say
their lovers strike in anger or dangle
like badly placed participles.

For the rest I had nothing left
to confide. No more tips
for terrific sex in language
of gourmet dinners or chitchat
on vaginas, foreplay, masturbation.
No more demos with hands
in televised close-ups on how to inspire
a diffident penis. Nothing appeased
the blind rut of autonomous desire,
its dunning ghostly like that of summer
locusts. Here in this small apartment

these mornings of calm
light it pleases me to play music,
gain back my lost passion
for painting. Windows face the water,
and hours each day I sketch patient
white angles of shore birds poised
always above only what is needed.

# Daisy

*My intention is to tell of bodies changed...*
—Ovid, *Metamorphoses*

This morning, picking daisies
for tonight's table and the friends
we have invited to dinner, I think
of you, Grandmother, named
by your parents over a century ago
in a small town west of Omaha
for this same, simple, most common
of blossoms. Did they note then
some likeness at your birth,
or know daisies were the latest
of Earth's flowers, thus a fit name
for their newborn daughter?

Ovid left no story about the daisy,
he who charms us to this day with tales
of gods transforming sordid deeds
into emblems of lasting beauty—
narcissus, nightingale, a tree of laurel.
At life's end he was no better
off than you: old, bitter, in exile
on the coast of the Black Sea,
far from the stir and glitter of Rome.
He lived the rest of his days
with fur-clad barbarians, denied
the velvet feel of Latin
on ear and tongue, hearing only
the graceless grunts of his savage
keepers and the strange language
of spiders that jabbered around him
in his hovel night and day.

In the rag bag of memory, the few
pictures of you that survive show
a fixed scowl ruling your face.
On the day of your wedding you frowned
into the camera, as if to say
the first bite of this promised sweet
tasted just as sour as the rest of life's
bitter table. No gods looking down
to watch as depression chiseled
away at you day after day. No gods
to pity your last breaths
as nursing home staff plucked
your few remaining petals:
Eastern Star ring, fake pearl necklace,
cheap wedding band, this last wrenched
until your gnarled finger broke,
bruising blue as a nosegay of asters.

No god next day by your casket
turning pain into the faintest
bloom of a smile. That job now
devolved to the undertaker.
A deft breaking of bones, skilled
rigging of pins and wires. Then,
with waxes and creams and glues,
with paints and powders and rose-
tinted lights, your mortal dross
morphed into memory's gold.

*—Some of the details of Ovid's exile have been adapted from David Malouf's* An Imaginary Life, *a fictional account of the poet's final years of exile in Tomis on the Black Sea.*

# After Watching Jacques Tati's *Mon Oncle*

*Hope was my uncle's middle name,*
*He died of it.*
—Linda Pastan, "The Five Stages of Grief"

Now and then, when I drive past a tavern
in early afternoon and see a solitary car
or two in an otherwise empty lot, I think
of you, Uncle, brought into our home
when I was ten to get you off the street.
You, hoping to face life square again

after the death of your young wife.
Two years I watched you try to keep your feral
thirst in check. You made yourself stay
busy with household tasks, small jobs that gave
a sense of use and your mind something
to chew on besides her life abruptly snatched.

One night late I found you passed out
in the dark of our tiny breakfast nook,
face down, drowning in a bowl of Mother's
thick bean soup. I drew you back
into the light you tried to evade
with drawn-out binges of cheap booze.

You liked pickled pigs' feet, liverwurst,
limburger cheese, and I prized the zany way
you cursed: *Hell-for-damn-boogerman-shit,*
you'd exclaim when you failed to roll a decent
cigarette from the little packet of cheap papers
and tobacco sack you were never without.

When you vanished, my parents said you snapped
and fled. *Back to Skid Row*, Mother said
with her usual rigid conviction. How easy
to confuse slipping into darkness with giving up.
I snooped to stay in touch as your story, bit
by bit, trickled in: The night you lit yourself on fire

after falling asleep smoking. The queue
of boozy women (*floozies,* Mother's preferred
term for them). The time you nearly lost
a hand scavenging food in a dumpster
behind your downtown cheap hotel (*fleabag,*
Mother called it). Father, when deep

in his cups, swore you didn't know shit
from Shinola, your ass from a donut's hole,
a few of his sayings that always left me
spinning to pin a tail on mute meaning's mule.
Still, I'd come home each day from school hoping
to find you rolling a smoke on our front porch swing

as you sang to our dog Boots or kibitzed
with pigeons roosting in our neighbor's eaves.
After Father edged up enough rungs at work,
we moved—nicer home, pricey school.
Time sped ahead, riding shotgun in our shiny new
Ford, but burred memories of you remained.

Then came news you'd died, had listed us
*Next of Kin.* Death, the nursing home caller said,
had come by steady subtraction, sugar in your blood
taking you slowly, limb by limb. Smoking, joking
right to the end, you kept the staff in stitches.
A real corker, the caller said, and sorely missed.

So today, when I pass a local tavern, on a whim
I stop in, order a stiff one, and lift a much overdue
glass to the few mid-day drinkers hunkered over
their shots and brews. *To my Uncle Floyd*, I say,
*who in fact knew shit from Shinola,*
*And chose it anyway.*

# Waterfront Concert

*—Houghton, Michigan*

This summer night the theme is memory
at the weekly concert, a cataract journey back
to the Era of Swing. After a day
of frazzling heat, a hint of cooling
in the air has brought half the town
down to the beach to unravel the frayed lines
of nostalgia and sway to the Big Band
beat of Benny Goodman, Count Basie, Duke
Ellington. We have come by water
and docked at the park's marina. The lake
is packed with a small fleet of pleasure
boats that seem to rise and fall at anchor
as one on amplified waves of music.
Jet skiers pester the Carvers and Chris Crafts
and Bayliners like fearless killer bees.
At our picnic table, strewn with the plastic
and Styrofoam debris of deli takeout and KFC,
some have caucused around gossip: the switchback
plot of a friend's failed marriage. The rest of us
have strayed to lawn chairs shaped
into a loose half-circle, where we can sip
beer and talk if we choose, or quietly sink
into the silt of an unaccountable sadness,
the kind that lurks on the boundaries
of each small joy. My eyes follow
a young man, stranded in childhood, a smile fixed
permanently on his face, one hand clutching
a soft drink, the other latched to his mother's.
His perma-press expression is familiar,
much like the one on my father after a vein
in his brain exploded. The mother gently coaxes

her blissful son down a gauntlet of soccer balls,
frisbees, and dancing couples. My parents danced
to these same tunes when I was still moored
in the safe berth of my mother's belly and war
had long since become more than just a rumor
on the world's tongue. She hummed these songs
like lullabies to soothe me through the swells
on her unbroken waters as she leaned
over a hot board ironing my father's shirts,
pressing the wrinkles out of those starched
white collars he wore like a priest to the office
to signal his holy devotion to work
he did for fifty years until the stroke reduced his part
to fool in a company of kings and petty thieves.
Up on the stand the band is now hot
into a very decent version of *Satin Doll.*
The young strut and shimmy their stuff.
A few of the old, stiff-limbed and gray
as the pestering flocks of gulls, rise
and almost imperceptibly sway, having come
to that place in a life where the un-danced melody
is almost far sweeter still. The sun
makes its obbligato way to the ridge
of hills off to the west. Soon we'll pack
our wicker baskets and lawn chairs back in the boat
and make our way across the dark lake,
still teething on a bone scrap of melody
or a half-remembered lyric. The lighted buoys
in the channel have already begun to blink
their simple rule of the sea at night: Green
to starboard if you wish to go farther,
red on right when you long to return.

# Another Day

The day from hell, the one you've been dreading,
begins with the peekaboo play of gray light
and the night's fourth call from your bladder.
Then the frenzied pizzicato of sparrows, juncos
in the branched bleachers outside the bedroom
window, and little whimpers of pain or pleasure
from your wife's last dream. Then, fitting no better
than the clothes you have planned for the day,
the news on public radio, right on cue, lays out
the night's pressed events: ideologies still locked
in their tedious tug of war, acts of terror
so stunning they demand the language of aesthetics,
another airliner plunging from the sky,
the voice of the pilot calm right up to the moment
he smacks into the wall of static.
You avoid the mirror as you complete your morning
ablutions, then confront a healthy bowl of mulch
for breakfast, one cup of coffee black and decaf
because your nerves of late have begun to smolder
and smell like fire in the wiring. In the car,
you're soothed by news of statistics that say
if you were going to have a heart attack today,
chances are you already would have had it.
Not long ago on your way to work you were routed
around a burning building. From miles away
you had seen the black snake of smoke whipping against
the blue sky, and flames in the full throttle
of their appetite. That's how you've come to think
about this day, but like all the rest it is over
fast enough, burning itself out over chatter and drinks
with your wife, a nice piece of fish, and the evening
paper's addenda: Someone you know is dead,

someone you envy is getting ahead, someone
you care for has been knocked silly by the sucker-
punching world. Soon you are back in bed, reading,
watching TV. Another day, and you have loved it
after all just as much as any other. Slowly sleep tightens
its boa grip, caressing your cheek with its unhinged lips.
Dreams swallow you whole and you rest
in the belly of the beast while outside in the trees
birds quietly tune their newly strung tongues
and fire walks your street in a hot pink leather skirt.

# Graffiti

Three friends in a bar, minus their wives,
not quite meeting each others' eyes as they talk, feeling
suddenly incomplete, the way you do when you lose
your keys or wallet and stand in a doorway
checking and rechecking each empty pocket, confusion
spreading over your face like cloud shadows racing
across open water. They come here a few weeknights
a year to lower consciousness, to watch the Lions
or Red Wings or Pistons, to drink quart beers, eat pickled eggs,
and knock it all down with a shot or two of whiskey.
Each would like to get beneath the surface of daily things
but floats mostly—sports, kids, work, the weather—
as if men were simply too much like cork ever to dive or sink
to deeper places women seem to reach as easily as fish.

After the second round they know without saying
it is time to go back to their porch-lit lives. They may want
to speak about happiness, luck, death, about the urge for sex
that lately has begun to fade in and out like a distant radio station
heard late at night when one is driving alone and full of joy
or sadness. They may want to ask how much the others argue
with their wives, with existence or God, but instead,
before leaving, they agree that they had all better *take a leak,*
as if somehow their plumbing itself revealed much deeper flaws
in their lives, and metaphor gave them a safe way to speak.

On the wall above one urinal, some Born Again,
believing even poor pissing sots deserve
second chances, has carefully printed: *Jesus Saves.*
Beneath, a local wit has scrawled *But Gretzky scores*
*on the rebound!* The three men laugh, as often they do
at the world's strange conjunctions, and in the bitter cold
outside they stand together for a moment, still laughing,

quoting other bits of graffiti that time had carved
on the walls of memory. Then they part to their separate cars,
each friend ready to drive slowly home through the snow
to a warm, loving other, the stars above them all the while
swarming like a power play about to form, perfect icons
of Chance, with its steady one-man advantage.

# I Hear Voices In A Book Shop In Duluth, Minnesota

It was offered in a slow and halting way,
as if the words had to be retrieved
from memory's Lost and Found.
*Books…are…like…old…friends:* that's what
he used to say, my teacher and friend,
on those days he came to class unprepared,
days that toward the end occurred more
and more. He would gently place a stack
of his dearest pals on the desk, gathered,
or so it seemed, at random from his cluttered office,
pick up the one on top, and off he would take
us on a purely improvised ramble,
wonderful journeys full of turns and twists
as if he were tweaking one of his favorite
quotes from Frost to say *No surprise*
*for the teacher, no surprise for the student.*
I heard his voice again this morning
as I bumbled bee-like among the blossoming
rows of a pleasant sun-lit bookshop.
Contrapuntal, my mother's voice chanted
in my other ear, her words bitter and elegiac,
how college and books had stolen me
from her and made me think I was better
than the rest of the family. And if it's true
that I lost my innocence not in the backseat
of my Buick but in the endless and musty stacks
of the university library, who can believe
the human story would ever have amounted
to much had not Eve and Adam selfishly
opted for the bitter fruit of knowledge?

And wasn't the apple simply a clever trope
for desire, which tells us to covet whatever
we haven't already got?

                                        Now in the bookstore
coffee shop, my pleasing stack of paperbacks
spread before me on the table like a Shibboleth,
a sign to the unlettered, I think happy thoughts
about original sin, about Satan, creation's
first Sophist. In an hour of browsing
I've lingered in Tuscan twilight with a bowl
of cold garlic soup and glass of Chianti,
bold yet unpretentious. I've unearthed good news
about butter and eggs, and coming closer
to the historical Jesus, I have found the old one
suits me better, and Buddha perhaps
better yet. Sipping my cappuccino, I admire
my new friends, their bright jackets,
their distinctive Garamond or Palatino dialects.
Beyond the glass window the unabridged edition
of the fallen world keeps turning its pages,
and I will be sorry to have to put it down.

*—for R. K. Meiners*

# At The Bishop Baraga Shrine

*—Keweenaw Bay, Baraga, Michigan*

In the fall, for the sake of sheer movement
and time alone, she'd come this far north from Florida,
land of Ponce de León, tracing U.S. 41
on her way to its source up in Copper Harbor.
Now this sculpted jut of chin, eyes of a raptor, staring
far out to where the bay meets Superior.
At the rest stop she'd seen the flier's imperative:
*See the Shrine of the Snowshoe Priest!*
Something in her had been piqued, if not curiosity
then perhaps needs which she had left unattended
for years. *Deus Absconditus, Deus Ex Machina—*
Since college she hadn't thought it really mattered.
Catholic but long since lapsed, she thought
this bronze cassock seemed no different
from the lampblack gowns of the grade school priests,
a wrap barely containing its messianic rut, useless,
she'd always thought, a matter of sheer waste
around which the sisters constantly clucked
and fussed, flirtatious brides of Christ engaged
in a chaste estrous dance. True, in her own way
she was something like a pilgrim, her motive
more modern, more profane—to save what might
yet be redeemed, though most of her heart had refused
to leave the galvanic thrum of Miami
for this lonely peninsula pointing across
a plumb-less expanse of lake like an arthritic finger.
She drops a few coins from her purse
into the box for donations, but as she begins to drift
absently back to the parking lot, some buried reflex
makes her turn back and kneel in the rustic grotto
before radiant rows of votive candles left by hosts
of summer visitors already gone before her.

Touching the wick to one of the transfixing eyes
of flame, she thinks suddenly of Pascal's wager,
and, like an agate picked up quite by chance
on a beach, her mind retrieves a melodious bit
of song, a TV ad from her childhood: *If everyone lit*
*just one little candle, what a bright world*
*this would be.* And because she does still believe
in the saving power of gesture, irony's inner
voice is little more than an insect's faint gossip
in her ear, a black fly's perhaps, which, she's heard,
no longer bites this late in the year.

# Slow-Pitch Tournament, Alston, Michigan

Sunday, mid-June, and the paper's lead story
on a local family and a DWI is a grave
reminder, if such were needed, we are all kin
to Socrates, and therefore must die.
But here in Alston even death and metaphysics
have turned more palatable with bratwurst, beer,
and near-perfect weather. A bracket tacked up
by concessions lists thirty teams in double elimination.
Just two—a scrub crew of local old-timers
and some college kids from a nearby town—
remain for the championship game. Losers gather
to stare at the bracket's absolute right
tracking logic, yet even loss is half
illusion here when there's always the next
weekend in L'Anse or Ontonagon.

Out along both foul lines behind snow
fences players and girlfriends or wives
drink Millers and Stroh's, complaining,
regretting their losses, but they know
there were plenty of reasons to lose,
and now unstrung muscles and sore arms
don't much matter, for somehow this milieu—
closed and precisely composed of forgiveness
and second chances—is what they've always needed
in a universe. The older players are young
enough still to win and remember.
There's a jigger of sun after winter
and hundreds of hearts chafing for base
hits or running one-hand catches.
Even two kids whisked away last night
by ambulance after being hit on their motorcycle
by a drunk driver are back stitched

and on crutches, clear proof if any were needed
this brief conjunction of space
and time has dispensed with rules.

Everyone says the leftfielder, who's five
for five, hides a bag under his loose uniform—
they don't know, cancer, maybe. They say
he's a hell of a guy, only twenty-nine,
a real fighter they say. In the last
of the ninth he slides on his side deep
down the line at the back of the warning
track to end the game. A thin membrane
of silence snaps when he rises, intact,
and no one thinks to stop clapping.

It's the infinite, fugitive moment
for the young winners, composed they say
mostly of Apostolics, non-drinkers,
but even that is believable here
in the dénouements of final beers and
mosquitoes. A ground crew retrieves bases.
Old, bruised heroes sprawl on car hoods,
drinking, rehearsing plays that did them in,
the ones that by winter will slide
toward myth. They are far from bitter
at the end of this familiar script
which soon takes them home to make love
to their women who all day have grown
steadily, suddenly more beautiful.

# Grass

*If you want me again look for me under your boot soles.*
—Whitman, *Leaves of Grass*

In past lives never one to putter in the yard,
tonight I join others up and down our new and pleasant
street at work rousing their lawns from the deep

inebriation of winter. The city plows have left
their annual legacy of sand, and as I rake I remember
my father pacing our barren acreage each spring,

rage scrawled in cursive across his face. Squalls
of anger blew from the bag of seed he carried in his maimed
hands—fingers and thumbs stubbed by dynamite

caps when he was a boy. I see him strike our land
like one of the wounded kings of myth, as if beating
and cursing the unresponsive earth might

make it yield and turn itself green again.
Twin maples kept his space, its fledgling blades
of grass, in day-long shade. Constant

parades of neighborhood children defeated
his deeply rooted needs for Nature, hope, passion,
and fruitful labor. Other things soon cast

their inhospitable shadows so that even the sod
he laid would not take, and he came to believe
in the camaraderie of dirt and water

his thirst with Seagram's. Tonight, he is a phantom
of pain in the scant turf beneath my feet. The sprinklers
up and down our dusk-defying street commence

their chant of *deep deep deep.* Each weed I pull
resists, and when it comes, it seems steeped in the venous
blood of this wild centrifuge, Earth.

# Word Games

Out on the deck things are falling
into place like the game of *Scrabble*
I play daily in my head to pit ruled words
against an unruly world. Only a few
letters remain, including the high stakes Zs

of course, but the locusts are turning
the latter into a scrim of pleasing ambient sound.
Drinks stand poured, steaks sputter
on the new gas grill, my wife drifts
beautifully among her phlox and daisies,

and our dog chews, atavistic, at a fake
bone as if it were the hip joint
of a freshly felled Yak. So I play
what I think is the day's final word:
*LUCK.* In tonight's paper, a *Newsmaker* item

about a man who thought the gun he stuck
in his mouth was empty. It was
meant as a joke for friends at a party.
Given my distance, it *is* a bit funny,
comedy being but one of many synonyms

for loss. By disposition my glass
is always half empty, so I top off
my drink and think about the gun,
the box of shells my father kept hidden
atop a cabinet in the breakfast nook.

How often did my brother and I fetch
the pistol down and take turns pointing it
at each other? *Bang! You're dead!* one of us
would shout, a trapped K at the back
of our palates making our trademark killing

sound. Each time we spun the cylinder
we too meant it as a joke. Each time
the chamber came up empty. And in truth
it *was* hilarious. Now my father is dead,
and my brother, and the poor schmuck

in tonight's column inch of filler and a rising
toll of others near or far in my memory,
and here I am, still sipping scotch and feeling
a bit lusty watching my wife bending
to her flowers. What truly last word to make

from such an unexpected stew of thoughts?
*DUMB*. Played off the U in *LUCK*.
For here am I, *mirabile dictu,* poor puny
surviving vowel, still pointing pearl-handled
words at a world plumb out of consonance.

# Confession

—*after* The Confession of Sin *in the Episcopal* Book of Common Prayer

Now, after years of willed
  silence, my mind kneels
    and I dial your number again.

No, I have not forgotten
  your trespasses. But before
    my season's warm days drift

away like an un-tethered party balloon,
  let me say it. As I listen
    to the splendid riff

of that cardinal resting
  like an open wound
    on the feeder, capped (still!)

with a late May snow,
  let me say it,
    my ears clear of irony

for the first time in years.
  Now, while the specks of blood
    in the specimen cup mean nothing

but the unidentifiable seed
  of another mystifying parable.
    Now, while grace still jingles

like a handful of change
  in my pocket, let me say it.
    Before that two-bit Angel

of Dying sends me
  on my knees up to the altar
    not from hunger

but fear, let me say it:
  I forgive.
    And I confess.

In word, in deed, most
  certainly in thought
    I have sinned. No

more, no less than you
  in your quicksilver moods:
    jealous, loving, wrathful.

And neither more
  nor less than the rest
    of this acquisitive world.

True. I have left much
  in the kingdom of the undone.
    I have loved nothing

with a whole heart, least
  of all myself. For all
    of this I repent. Delight

in your will? The best
  I can muster—Acceptance.
    Walk in your ways?

A small light would be
  useful. If I regret this life
    is not now as it was

in the beginning,
  let it end when
    (and as) you see fit.

As it must: back to ashes,
  back to a fist full of dust. With
    or without Amen. *Amen.*

# The Fisher King At The Mayo Clinic

*The Fisher King, keeper of the Holy Grail, has a genital wound that has destroyed his virility. When he is injured, his kingdom suffers as he does, his impotence affecting the fertility of the land and reducing it to a Wasteland. Little is left for him to do but fish in the river near his castle. Knights from many lands try to heal the Fisher King but only the chosen can accomplish the feat.*
—Encyclopedia entry

1.

All he sees at first, stepping
from the chartered jet onto the tarmac,
are rolling fields that seem aflame
in sunlight angled from the west,
and then the Clinic, its gleaming turrets
rising in the distance above vast tracts
of parched corn like Mecca
or the unbreached towers of Troy.

2.

A quick ride by limo and soon
he is settled in the royal suite to await
tomorrow's tests and teams of doctors
in richly tailored suits. Over a bland dinner
he thinks of home, of his own castle,
where the Queen now broods alone
in her separate chambers. How long now
since he woke to find desire
reduced to nothing more than a whisper
deep in his loins, sighing like dry wind
across infinite reaches of sand?

3.

Watching television, his mind turns
once more to the Grail he guarded
so long and well the world lost interest,
its mysteries freeze-dried into pulp
and celluloid fictions. On cable news
he sees his sickness spreading far
beyond his tiny kingdom: the world's
cisterns empty, cattle bloated
and dying, rivers dry, wildfires
unchecked, their smoke turning
the sky opaque as the eyes
of blind soothsayers.

4.

Day after day, more tests, more waiting.
Afternoons, ambulatory, he plays
a grand piano in the polished lobby,
and always, from the thick current
of stricken, a few pause to listen,
surprised at the sound of living
music, grateful for this brief distraction
from their own compacted grief.

5.

Almost daily, farmers, bankers, sheiks
shuffle to a square of open floor,
some alone, cradling their canisters
of oxygen like shy partners, others
swaying together in scrums
and loose half circles, as if their bodies
heeded some deep limbic need for dance.

Such times he leans harder into the keys,
as if these skeins of improvised notes
might shatter the lobby's vaulted glass
ceiling, soar high above the steel towers
that shimmer in unrelenting heat,
and compel the sky's brow to darken
at last with a resurrecting rain.

6.

Nights, caught in the undertow
of sedated dreaming, he limps down
each evening to his river that runs full
once more. With rod, reel, and a jeweled box
of tiny, artful flies he wades far out,
toward deep pools, where sleek trout
are rising to a hatch of stars.

# The Evil Eye

*Can any hide himself in secret places that I*
*shall not see him? saith the Lord.*
—Jeremiah 23:24

In the busy Greek commerce of the Plaka
I stop before a rack of sky blue
glass eyeballs wedded to tiny silver
chains—potent charms, the shop keeper

explains, to nullify the power of the Evil Eye.
My mind leaps back to the baleful glower
of my grandmother's rooster:
how it fixed me with its crazed glare

through a single hexagon of chicken wire.
The precise piercing look Preacher Pinkerton
railed about Sundays at the Baptist church,
spitting admonitions at me from his lofty perch

about the all-seeing eye of God—an x-ray
stare that could bore, he fervently swore,
straight through to the very marrow
of my sinful bones. By nature

shy, my adolescent face disgraced
by acne, I felt the vast world gaping
at me, and God first among the worst
of the steadfast gawkers. At first I tried

keeping my eyes open when I prayed,
but my skin continued to blush and burn
from His unrelenting gaze. Finally,
I simply turned away. At bedtime, I'd hang

a *Closed* sign on the imagined little booth
where for years I kneeled each night to pray.
By day I'd draw the drapes and shutters tight:
Out of mind, out of omnipresent sight.

For years I tried to hide that way. Now here,
at this street-side stall in sun-bleached Athens,
ancient gods of the Acropolis peering
down through blinding heat, I pick one

of the bright blue amulets, slip it
in my pocket next to my string of worry
beads. Thus armed, I sally forth back
into the Plaka's thick pedestrian traffic.

I've edged past my allotted number of noons.
Time, my sparrow's heart: Both have kept
up their implacable ticking away. My booth,
so long deserted, will need a fresh coat of paint,

but most of all, plain and visible, a sign:
*Under New Management...Coming Soon.*

# Dickering With God

An hour ago the phone yanked my wife
and me from sleep. My Cry Wolf heart
tom-tommed in my chest: Someone we love—
a son, a sister—surely dead or mangled
on a gurney in Intensive Care. When I answered,
a voice said, *Is Artie there?* Nerves aquiver,
I shouted: *You have the wrong number!* Peeved, pissed,
I hissed: *It's 3 a.m.!* A pause, then: *This is Vernon. I'm lost.*
I was about to quip *Who isn't?* when I heard
the hang-up, felt the deep silence of disconnection.
*Wrong number,* I grumbled to my wife and doused
the bedside lamp, my heart still punching
against the walls of my chest like some wild thing
trussed up in a gunny sack.

Now, still wide awake,
my mind churning like the little color wheel
on my laptop, I recall other sleepless nights
in the Way Back of Time when I lay tucked
in fetal prayer: *Give me my biblical three score
and ten,* I pleaded, an age that seemed impossible
then because any moment I might die.
*Don't walk up a steep hill in a cold wind,*
the doctor had warned as he flipped shut
my chart and fixed me with a Sibyl's eyes.
How quickly the world pivots toward the Absurd.
I was a bit shy of 30. Just as Camus predicted.
And what more purely absurd than thinking
about one's own death? Deeply in love
with myself, I begged: *Get me to 70. I promise
I'll ask for nothing more.*

Tomorrow I turn 74,
look forward to presents, ice cream, cake.
Gravity pulls more strongly now. My knees ache.
The ones I metaphorically bend each night
have stayed somewhat supple as I've begun
again to dicker with God. In truth, more filibuster,
more pitch than prayer. Don't those late-night ads
on TV for this or that amazing gizmo cut straight
to the quick of it? The deep human hunger for *More.*
Always *More.*

Here, in the dark,
snow and wind buffeting the house, I can't shake
Vernon's voice, the straight, simple way he confessed
to being lost. *Lord God, I have no idea where*
*I am going:* So prayed Thomas Merton, knowing
neither the road ahead nor his own core self.
Call back, Vernon. This time I will listen.

# Mortician's Advice Regarding The Hands

At open caskets, when they can't bear to look
   into the face of the deceased, mourners turn
to the hands. They hold or stroke them. They kiss
   what clung to a mother's breast, caressed

a lover's body, struck out in anger, or tented
   tautly in prayer. Hands that once spoke
the complex language of touch. If a child, staring
   at hands badly caked with makeup, asks

*What gets on you when you die?* you've failed.
   First, foremost, hands, once you've finished,
must never look dead, but simply at rest,
   with just the slightest illusion of movement.

When you've brought them back to life,
   made them look better than your own, pause,
breathe, feel satisfied. Then move on
   to the nails. Repair any damage

with acrylic, then file each with meticulous care.
   An almond shape works best, making hands seem
longer, slimmer. Savor your absence of haste.
   Pause again. Step back. Admire your work.

Then apply polish. Do not be afraid of color.
   Applied in even layers, it makes perfect
the seam between finger and nail, an important
   detail sorrow's eyes require. Be tireless

as grief itself in your quest for perfection.
  At their core, finished hands, like architecture,
harmonize form and space. Close your eyes.
  Visualize. Then lay one revived hand chastely

across the other just above the waist. Drops
  of Superglue work best to hold them firmly
in place. Step back. Behold. Yours is never art
  for art's sake. During the service, stand

against the rear wall, inconspicuous.
  Clasp your hands behind your back. Finger
your own nails discreetly. Make note
  of each and every flaw. As the grieving leave,

some will pause to praise your work.
  Show gratitude and grace. Then book
the best salon in town. Do not wait.
  When the manicure is finished, luxuriate.

Memorize that feeling of perfect hands.
  Deface them before your next shift.

*—A mostly found poem derived from the website* The Order of the Good Death

# The Recovery Room

This is where they bring you
when the knife has finished
its work, when that small army
of hands has quelled
the sudden riot
in a distant province of your body.
Here your breath must learn
to stand again on its own
two lungs, your heart
prove it can still carry on
its own steadfast little tune.
Here memory must forget
its losses, your tongue remember
your name, your date of birth.
Beneath the blaze of lights
you see the masked faces
leaning over you, and at last
hear their invitation to awake.
There is the priest, still clutching
the tiny vial of oil in his pocket.
You will not need it.
The world is, once again,
a breast swollen with milk.
Drink deeply. Put that other
hunger behind you. Your placc
at the table has been saved.

# Wait For Me

The wind has nothing to offer
  this morning but sleep. Mid-August,
the nights cooler now, and snow
  already piling up in our imaginations.

The garden, fortunately, has no memory,
  and grows heavy with beans, tomatoes.
A small harvest, but we are grateful
  for this pocketful of change

from the earth, to which, surely
  as the wind blows and tomatoes ripen,
the body will return, its pockets
  empty, its loans paid off and clear.

What is this morning wind
  but freed spirits, long waiting,
impatient now? Whatever comes,
  we must wait for one another.

Where? In that small patch of woods
  by the lake. Whoever is first, heart
filling with offshore breeze: Stay.
  Tethered there until the other is free.

*—for J. B.*

# Dancing School

This morning rising from the basement,
stomping cold from my shoes, I see
gray footprints traced on kitchen tiles
from where I have just left off stoking
the wood-fueled furnace. Winter mornings
my father left such ashy traces when he rose
up from tending coal while we boys dozed

over cod liver oil and little boats of fried corn
mush afloat in pools of Karo syrup.
So I have followed in his footsteps after all,
as if we had been partners all along
in one of those dance-by-mail schools
where you learn each new sequence
from footprints pasted in rhythmic

patterns across the hardwood floor.
In this my 74th year, beyond, as I am
now his own last dance, I still feel like new
wine. My final bottle? Perhaps. Better
savored than saved. One last slow dance
with Dionysus. Years ago, at a fold in my life,
with reasons to be sad and alone, I stood

on a balcony in the atrium of a pricey hotel
and watched far beneath me graceful couples
at a Tea Dance, teachers and students,
as I recall, of an Arthur Murray school,
exotic flurry of feathers, sequins, tuxedoed poses,
polished products of self-conscious practice,
step by tedious painted step: rhumba,

fox trot, bossa nova. It was dreamy, unreal,
like that dance scene in Bertolucci's
*Last Tango in Paris*, the couples below
so stylish I very nearly forgot
Brando's violence with butter and sex.
My friends and I dance less often now,
but because we have been through it

a long time together, some nights—
New Year's Eve perhaps—when need rises
in us like hunger's sacrament, we dance,
twos or threes or fives or even alone,
our bodies like small scrums of prayer,
doxologies of gratitude and grief for those
we love—present, passed—our lives now

slowly, steadily returning to that first school
dance long ago where we pressed ourselves shyly
by gender against opposing walls, divided
by nothing but space, music, dimmed light,
and tongues tied into knots by unspoken desire.
This morning these ashy traces my feet leave
say I am still moving. So while my wife

stares, her buttered toast paused mid-air,
I move, hot and nimble and raw as aching
knees and creeping years allow, jiving
to a new tune, one getting a lot of play
of late in my head: great lyrics, a good beat
you can really dance to, better now,
if only for knowing the score.

*—for Jack Driscoll*

# About the Author

Randall R. Freisinger's poems have appeared in various anthologies and numerous literary magazines such as *New Letters, The Chariton Review, Sugar House Review, South Carolina Review, Atlanta Review, Black Warrior Review, Tar River Poetry, Green Mountain Review, Cream City Review, Xavier Review, Pank, Marlboro Review, Passages North,* and many others. Nominated for a Pushcart Prize seven times, he has four collections of poems: *Running Patterns* (1985 Flume Press National Chapbook Competition winner), *Hand Shadows* (Green Tower Press Chapbook Series, 1988), *Plato's Breath* (May Swenson Poetry Prize, Utah State University Press, 1997), and *Nostalgia's Thread: Ten Poems on Norman Rockwell Paintings* (chapbook, Hol Art Books, 2009).

Born and raised in Kansas City, MO, he holds B.J., M.A., and Ph.D. degrees from the University of Missouri-Columbia. In 1983-84 he was Visiting Scholar in poetry in the University of Massachusetts-Amherst's M.F.A. Program. He lives and writes in Michigan's Upper Peninsula, where he is Emeritus Professor of Rhetoric, Literature, and Creative Writing in the Department of Humanities at Michigan Technological University.

Made in the USA
Coppell, TX
10 May 2020

24609883R00072